CALLED TO THE PRIESTHOOD

The author's royalties from this book are being donated to "Aid to the Church in Need".

CALLED TO THE PRIESTHOOD

George Osman

NEW HORIZON

ISBN 0 86116 714 7

Printed & Published by
NEW HORIZON
Horizon House
5 Victoria Drive
Bognor Regis
Sussex.

CALLED?

My fifty-five years as a priest emboldens me to produce this serious booklet, instead of indulging in my favourite pastime - writing an amusing novel. My wits are, I believe, quite sound. Certainly my memory is good.

Although amusing incidents may be reported, my purpose is to challenge any Christian man to face up to a question. There is a shortage of clergy. IS GOD CALLING YOU TO THE PRIESTHOOD?

As the call may come to ANY MAN, I have deliberately refrained from naming places and all but historical characters. But the facts recorded are, to the best of my belief, quite true.

To any man who hears the call through these pages I would also say, "You have been warned." God's call is serious.

"Do you think in your heart, that you be truly called - to the Order and Ministry of Priesthood?" (Anglican Ordinal 1662).

He who responds should found his work upon our Lord - not upon his personal popularity, gimmicks, hopping on the "Band Wagon", of passing avant-garde notions in theology or politics. Above all he must build upon whatever was sound in teaching and practice of those whom he succeeds in Office and never claim that he alone is responsible for all the success.

1 Cor. Chap 3
St. Mark 8, 34

I "Train up a child in the way he should go; and when he is old, he will not depart from it."

Proverbs xxii, 6.

It seems clear that St. Paul's Timothy was a "Once Born" Christian unlike the great Apostle, not needing that kind of conversion which led to St. Paul's New Birth, having the same unfeigned faith as his grandmother Lois and his mother Eunice. Happily, some of us are in that group, brought up as Christians from childhood, our answer to God's Call being continuous. But nowadays this Call may come to more people suddenly, due to the climate of the times. They suddenly experience a flash of light which brings wisdom. My scientist son-in-law found wisdom, not at his Confirmation, which meant little, but at London University.

Unhesitantly, I class myself with the "Once Born". Perhaps we are apt to be smug. Though I was not conscious of it, the village schoolboys certainly thought so.

My father retired from his post as head teacher of a church school before he was fifty, on inheriting a legacy. An old man when I was born, he came of a good family fallen on evil days through his ancestor's evil ways. Our home was orderly, decorous in every way and happy. But "children must be seen and not heard".

Our incumbent was disabled by arthritis, "poor as a church mouse" in his "Starving" benefice, but generous to a fault. Father was his right-hand man; Correspondent of the

National School of Managers, choirmaster, rector's church-warden; as disciplined in bearing and language as his parish priest could sometimes be rash.

This parson of an able mind took Dean Swift as his model. Father found him acceptable in that he gave definite tractarian teaching. For instance, he appeared in the village school daily to teach the older boys and girls Scripture and the Church Catechism. The latter we had to learn by heart, both question and answer, and I took pride in winning the first prize by making only one spelling mistake in the "Finals". He diligently hobbled around to visit those whom my father had reported as unwell, using the "Order for the Visitation of the Sick" and giving "The Last Rites" to the dying. But he was not given to ceremonial and was "slap-dash" in conducting church services.

He aggravated my father, a keen Conservative, by being a Radical and tactless in expressing such views in the pulpit. So much so that the Tory Agent was heard to say, "Damn the parsons." Yet, he was snobbish towards all his parishioners but my family.

....

Other influences at work in my Christian upbringing include that of a devout nursemaid who had a great respect for her own village priest and, of course, my mother. Her motto seems to have been:-

"In wisdom let us grow
As years and strength are given
That we may serve Thy Church below
And join Thy Saints in heaven."

I am sure that she prayed for me much as St. Monica did for her son, St. Augustine of Hippo, and had her heart's desire fulfilled when I became a clergyman.

My own first thought of the Ministry came, oddly enough, when mother was decorating the pulpit for the "Feast of St. Pumpkin and the Blessed Vegetable Marrow". I was then about eight years old and had climbed the stairs and stood there in silence for quite a long time, wondering????

By this time I had spent about one year at the village school, where the children were most uncouth, the moral tone and manners shocking, indecency prevalent. So much was this in evidence that our liberal-minded rector withdrew his own son hurriedly. I was as then very shy, hesitant in speech, and held my head to one side. My quiet and unassertive bearing at first called forth the chorus, "Look at sloping Jesus. 'Ee never swears." I merely grinned and said nothing.

Since my retirement, I have lived with my elder daughter and her family. Turning over some old family photographs, I noticed that my eldest grandson faced the camera in an even more shy fashion by tucking his head down to his knees when a small boy. One of my two sons also behaved in exactly the same way, so this shyness is not due to a child's upbringing.

....

We were offered such excellent general education in that school, if we took advantage of it, that although only classed as "one of his mediums" by the head teacher, I passed out at the top of county examination for a free scholarship to a grammar school. The school chosen by my parents was an old one of Church foundation. The Head was, therefore, ipso facto, a churchman. Ours had been Vice-Principal of the local Church Training College for teachers and held a first-class Doctorate in science.

Founded, exactly like Eton, as a "Charity school", it had not become (like Eton) mainly a school for rich children. The school was comprehensive in accepting boys of all grades of society and ditto in numbering dunces and able pupils upon its roll. A very humble public school, charging small fees, most of us were sons of the lower paid professional men and of a few discerning manufacturers who valued the excellent teaching in secular subjects.

It may therefore be plain to readers that little preparation was given to fit pupils for most "learned professions", the only obvious opening on leaving the sixth form was to become a schoolmaster. One or two boys did become accountants or lawyers. But most of us, like myself, were drafted into the Science Sixth. There was I at sixteen and was soon made a "Pupil teacher" in a slum, where I learned to teach every morning and worked in the laboratory every afternoon. My experiences in that slum school proved valuable twenty years later.

It is an understatement to say that the Christian influence in grammar school was negative. Apparently bored assistant masters leaned against the walls at "Morning assembly", as the devout head master led us in an act of worship. The "Scripture master", a Methodist, was reverent and sincere. I remember him chiefly because he asked the class on one occasion which of us were Church of England choristers. His reaction to our replies was, "Well, all the class will learn Psalm 104 in the Authorised Bible Version."

....

During the above period, our rector moved and the new priest was a definite Anglo Catholic. He taught me to serve the Altar, about Confession (valuable later), and instilled religious discipline. All was performed "decently and in order". This man possessed little learning, but tried to live in "sanctified poverty" like the Curé d'Ars. He served as a Confessor to several local learned people.

After the outbreak of the 1914 war, he took me to a Sung Requiem Mass for the Fallen. My first contact with Catholic ceremonial, simple though it was and of the Prayer Book Order, made a great impression upon me. As an example of discipline to which I assented without a murmur, try to beat this: Sunday Holy Communion 8 a.m. serve: teach Sunday School 10 a.m.: Sing Matins with the choir 11 a.m.: teach Sunday School 2.30 p.m.: sing Evensong with the choir 6.30 p.m.

II "Wisdom can only be truly tested among the pressures and pitfalls of our daily living." (Thoughts from Bible Reading Fellowship Notes.)

War dragged on and when I reached the age of seventeen and a half, I volunteered and joined the Royal Navy Volunteer Reserve. Because of my scientific training I began as a Wireless Operator. Despite the repugnant barrack room conversation, the little "flame of the holy fire" was kept alight. Influence for good came from a sternly moral friend, who slapped my face for one of my indecent remarks, and from the Senior Chaplain - despite the evil influence of his sacristan, a filthy beast. The few regulars at Holy Communion were entertained from time to time at the chaplain's house.

Everybody paraded on Sundays at "Divisions", where the Chaplain was given the "grand salute". Petty Officers saluted their Lieutenants, these passed the salute up to the Commander, he to the Commodore and from thence it went to the Chaplain as he came forward to recite the prayers. And "when the 'oly man sez, 'Let us pray', then it's 'ats orf", came in a stage-whisper from our P.O.

To the serried ranks assembled for the mid-morning parade, a Chief Petty Officer might yell; "Church of England stand at ease. Roman Catholics fall in on the right. Fancy religions to the rear. Dismiss." So thousands would march to our C. of E. service. It did them no harm and "sailors don't care".

The Assistant Chaplain, an evangelical of some sort, held Mission Services. There we were called to "Stand up for Jesus" and I must confess that it went against the grain to lay bare my soul in that kind of way, though I went up to him afterwards and accepted a prayer card. That seemed quite decent. At least I needed to remember those words I had so often sung, "Make me a clean heart, O God: and renew a right spirit within me".

Passing out as a trained W.T. Operator, I was sent to gain experience by assisting a senior man in a wooden herring drifter operating from its base on the East Coast. The vessel's job was to lead a small squadron of these tiny craft in mine-sweeping and convoy work. Our skipper was not able to read nor write, but he knew his way about that part of the North Sea merely by the sound of the moving water, We carried, as we were the Flagship, a R.N.R. Lieutenant who was the second officer of a liner in peace time.

The crew of ten more were foul-mouthed fishermen, passing few remarks which lacked sexual undertones - sometimes blatant filth. Kindly and surprisingly God-fearing, they respected the Church and gladly marched on parade to an "advanced" type of place. Afterwards they might even discuss the sermon.

While serving there, I met another youthful assistant telegraphist who asked my advice about his misuse of his sexual instincts. One Sunday evening I attended Vespers at the local R.C. Church and, for the first time, heard a sermon about "One flock, one shepherd" and prayers for Christian Unity.

In the middle of my two months' service there, we suffered such a buffeting in the mad March gales while out in the North Sea that we ran for harbour to have the damage repaired and I enjoyed a week's leave and strengthened my hold upon home and its influence.

....

Service on the drifter was followed by a few weeks at our huge naval barracks to complete W.T. training and then be sent on further service. I never met any chaplains, remember no religious services, there might as well have been nothing of the sort. No real contact was attempted with us, under a barrage of indecent language and suggestion, open to the danger of homosexuality at the hands of at least one naval policeman. Almost too much for an eighteen year old to face. Certainly not lower the age of consent.

Conclusion - Religious influence negative!

On the completion of this course, two of us were posted to a "Hush Hush" station on an island in Orkney. There was no Anglican Chaplain anywhere near. One Leading Telegraphist, a Roman Catholic with most amusing travel tales, set a good example in never blaspheming even when at his filthiest spate of "language". The Chief Officer was nominally C. of E., as were all the others but one member of The Church of Scotland. Regarding attendance at a place of worship,

"They cared for none of these things".

This group of a dozen men let me alone, but might not have done so had I knelt by my bedside and prayed aloud. They did not make fun of me for attending the Scottish United Free Church services from noon to 2 p.m. when off duty. On the whole they were a very decent crowd and included civil engineers, a bank clerk, a solicitor's clerk, an ex-public school boy chartered accountant - that is in peace time - and three regular R.N. ratings.

The minister at the U.F. Church conducted a very tedious service. But I brightened up the proceedings by repairing the wheezy harmonium and playing it. He was most delighted and made me blush at the way he spoke of me as a "Member of the High Kirk of England" who had done the congregation such a favour and regularly represented the wireless station at their services.

My reason for attending that particular church was on account of my friendship with a small laird, who kept a shop and ran the Post Office. He told me that he felt that I had been sent to replace his son who had died not long before, and being entertained at his house for a meal after the service deepened my link with that family and their Edinburgh relations. Above all I felt great benefit from it.

My year in Orkney was not particularly adventuresome, though it had its moments. I left with mixed feelings when the influence of a certain nobleman set wheels in motion and I was suddenly hustled off home to prepare to enter a Cambridge college.

III "Wisdom is a grace of character which blossoms through trials and does not wither in the sunshine of rewards." (Thoughts. B.R.F.)

At nineteen years of age I met the aged head of my Cambridge college and was surprised to find he was acquainted with my father, having been the Principal of the Teachers' Training College previously mentioned. He was thus, indirectly linked with my old school.

Compulsory chapel was no burden to me. I only occasionally went to hear the university sermon. But the music at King's Chapel was a great attraction. Of religious influence there was a surfeit. Take it or leave it. C.I.C.C.U. (Kick You) - Evangelical, scored one attendance. This was through the earnest entreaty of one member who went round asking, "Are you saved?" In those days I knew, like Shakespeare, a little Latin and less Greek, so I could not ask as I should have done after studying Greek - "Sozo, the root Greek word from which conjugations appear in the Scriptures, can mean at least three conditions. Which of these do you mean? For example, I am in the position of being saved, hope I am in the state of salvation, but am not yet finally saved. Then, saved from and for what? My friend study your Greek Testament and let me alone."

The poor fellow I have mentioned was so aggressive that we all tried to avoid sitting next to him in Hall or we might choke over our dinner. Strangely enough, he was a scholar of the college unless I am confusing him with the chap whose turn came to read the Lessons and incredibly read the names of the "Three Children" in Daniel as "Shadrach, Meshach, and Abendigo", whereas the last is clearly Abed-nego.

We all grew accustomed to being asked about the state of our souls. I found it a different matter when F. Buchman, no less a person I feel sure, asked me a question that seemed more indecent than some of the "language" I had heard. "My friend, do you masturbate?" or words to that effect. It was at a period of "Moral Rearmament", but nasty.

Through friendship with an Anglo-Catholic son of a parson, I was introduced to the pleasures of Gilbert and Sullivan and also was a member of S.T.C., a society directly opposite to "Kick You". But when its chairman, the head of one of the colleges, resigned I also gave up attending. Members were more concerned with "spiky" ceremonial and dressing up than with the discipline which I still consider an essential.

Our frail chaplain at college was replaced by one from the trenches. So this priest who had heard a soldier on the duckboards say "Quiet Bill with yer swearin'. This is the bloody Vicarage", popped out his head from the dug-out "Vicarage" and exclaimed, "And here's the bloody vicar." He became a much loved Dean and later Master.

From hindsight I am sure I ought to have read Honours Theology. But our school head was an eminent scientist, so up for the Natural Sciences Tripos was I sent. My director of studies was pleased with my work over the full year I had spent, after settling down and doing little in that Summer Term, called May Term, free from the Navy. Therefore I sat the second year honours examination and was told I had reached Class II standard and was due to sit my Finals after another year. So I had studied for only two full years instead of three.

In addition to my scientific studies, I spent leisure hours on the running track and in swimming. I also felt drawn to study Divinity and attended the university professors' lectures in this subject, thereby obtaining "Divinity Testimonials", which were then all that was needed to be considered a worthy candidate to be Ordered Deacon.

All appeared to be going well during that final year. Then, just before my twenty-first birthday, my father died of a stroke after lying helpless for three months, my mother suffered increasingly from fits - afterwards diagnosed as due to diabetes - and I became increasingly worried until I was on the verge of a mental breakdown. The result of the final examination, when it was expected that I should do well, was almost complete failure.

Looking back, this catastrophe does not surprise me. I had spent two years in the Science Sixth Form, half of it practising teaching. Nearly two years of study had been almost wasted in the Navy and science had meanwhile been advancing so fast that much of my knowledge was out of date. In the examination hall I was unable to marshal my thoughts I could scarcely spell simple words and in the laboratory the specimen I examined, blew up in my face. What could be done?

A theological college had already accepted me that summer, no doubt meaning what one tutor said, "We are glad to welcome another Dr. Barnes." Although I did not take this as a compliment, I was very kindly accepted despite my failure and, after reading for the ordinary degree in Theology, was eventually able to add "B.A." after my name a year later.

In the meantime, my tutor in the university had sent for me and told me what a fool I had been not to report the trouble I had passed through and the shocking state of my mind. He said that an aegrotat honours degree had often been granted for less reason.

This humiliation was a sort of "negative call", a halt to the march in a direction not intended for me, namely a scientific career. I think we can reverently compare such guidance with that of St. Paul, "Forbidden by the Holy Spirit to preach the Word in Asia".

Although the wearing of brief shorts at tennis was not then "de rigeur", quite the reverse, I used my athletics gear to save buying "whites". Money was scarce after my father's death. I could not even afford to buy books needed for study and although living simply was soon in debt. For my "indecency" at tennis and my debts I was sternly upbraided by the principal, who wrote to my widowed mother. On receipt of a cheque by return of post and being told in no uncertain terms that it was his duty to take care of his students, I was welcomed that day to supper with his family.

By this time I had decided to set to work to repay the loan from the kindly chaplain, who believed that "Faith without works is dead". When offered the post of science master at a good school on the South Coast and another at a Musical College Preparatory School, an evangelical friend, whose morals in such matters were not above reproach, piously advised me against teaching in a choir school.

I have no objection to prayer meetings, as such, but this man had taken me to one in which I was referred to as "our sinful brother". You can imagine the "Aye-mens" and gasps of horror when I offered a prayer for God's forgiveness of the awful sin of spiritual pride and self-righteousness. So his advice went unheeded and I was appointed as second master of the college and took up residence after a long holiday in which I taught a lazy but intelligent youth well enough to get him through the London Matriculation Examination. There, entertained by his family, I was quite at home in an Anglo-Catholic atmosphere.

IV "The fear of the Lord, that,
that is wisdom. And to depart
from evil, that is understanding."
(Words of anthem, often sung at the
college. See Job xxviii,28.)

Richly endowed, the college had once been attended by sons of the gentry. In my days sons of the clergy, of better class tradesmen and of well-to-do farmers were taught there to prepare them for entry into public schools.

No indecency between masters and boys was evident, though it had occurred some years before. What was apparent was the sort of backbiting to be found among a staff with not enough work to do. There were seven teachers coping with fifty boys.

The music was delightful, ceremonial mildly catholic - we sang the Eucharist on Sundays and daily Matins and Evensong to a Cathedral type of Service, rather better singing than most of them.

During my first happy year, I was interviewed by the bishop and prepared for his chaplains' examination, passing it easily. My being made a deacon occurred in the college chapel, where an Oxford professor acted as the "Gospeller" and I was "presented" to the bishop by an asthmatic canon in a screech which set our choristers giggling. My "title" was with the College Warden and my troubles began. The warden was the administrative head of the establishment and the final authority. Unfortunately this authority was delegated in part to the teaching headmaster and this division of power led to constant friction. This was aggravated by the warden's kindly, but weak, ineffective character. Later, I was in a position to advise the Fellows of the college to unite the posts of warden and headmaster. This was done and there is little trouble of that sort today.

At the beginning of the following year our head was given a living and a new man appointed. He seemed to me to be an insufferable snob, scornful of me and what I call "nit picking" at me with mock facetiae. As his pinpricks did not work, he determined to oust me and at the end of my second year there, a pathetic letter arrived from the warden during the Easter holidays, begging me to resign for the sake of peace.

My bishop told me that I could not be thrown out as I was licensed to the place. The choice was mine, whether to leave or remain. The following year I was told by the warden that he had rid himself of the troublesome head and wished I had stayed in his place.

However, I chose to depart and was sent to serve under a lovable, though choleric archdeacon. This rector of a small town taught me my job, largely by letting me alone in charge of a tiny village church. After spending a week or two in visiting every house in the place, we had a church full, with the squire and his little orchestra leading the plain-chant singing. I also visited a town district and we met weekly à la famous Portsea to report to the rector on our work.

At the end of two happy years my rector

sent for me and said "Dear man (his usual form of greeting), I am leaving this parish to take up my residentiary canonry. It is only right that a new priest should hold this good living. I don't need the money. Perhaps you may want to move."

During this period I had, of course, passed my priest's examinations and was duly ordained and friendly with the bishop's son. Again, I should leave with mixed feelings. But my mother's health was worse and I had a letter from an old acquaintance, a Fellow of the college. His letter read, "I have read that your rector is leaving the parish and 'nothing venture, nothing have'. Will you come and be my colleague?"

I told my bishop of the matter and he said that my friend's bishop would be at a certain function at our Cathedral in the following week and that he would introduce me to him. The conversation went like this, "Bishop, this man has been offered a senior curacy in your diocese with Mr. so-and-so. He is a good priest and I should be sorry to lose him."

"Well, well. He's welcome to come. But if any work is done there after his arrival, I shall know who is responsible."

....

Settled in this new work, I found that my rector and I had mutual friends in the East Midlands as well as the founder of the "Guild of St. Nicholas" (now styled the Royal School of Church Music) and our connection with the musical college of which he soon became sub-warden.

Undeterred by the frank remarks of my new bishop, quoted at the end of the previous section, I set to work visiting the greater part of the parish. Working upon the principle that "a house-going parson makes a church-going people", I undertook the task as laid down by the dear old archdeacon. Using a note book for every street, I made a directory of residents, adding secret signs to indicate whether they had been baptised, went to church or elsewhere, were communicants and so forth.

The timid rector left me to deal with rough or quarrelsome people and to settle troubles, besides training the choir, youth work and most of the preparation of candidates for confirmation. I persuaded him to organise a band of district visitors who also distributed parish magazines and met monthly to collect them and inform us of persons who needed a call from us. The rector usually visited the sick when he hoped they were recovering. "That was much more pleasant."

The district, into which I "dug", to quote the archdeacon, was very largely a continually growing housing estate. In this part of what is now a huge parish, I celebrated Holy Communion fifteen years later for the new vicar on a Wednesday at 7.30 a.m. and found over forty young communicants in attendance before they went off to their daily work. Obviously he had built well upon something sound in the foundations that had been laid - the only wise method of Christian Ministry.

Another fifteen years on, and a lovely church stood in that district which had been a mere heath when I had first arrived forty years before. Even now, many people whose names I have forgotten, greet me when I visit the place. "More know Tom Fool than Tom Fool knows."

....

Our dean and chapter offered me a benefice in the north of the country after I had ministered for six years as a curate, so I became the rector of two small villages. Fortunate in succeeding an old Tractarian canon, I had no difficulty in introducing a monthly Sung Eucharist for the Sunday School and its parents and said daily morning and evening prayer to the amusement of some ignorant or waggish parishioners. I was in no hurry to teach the use of much ceremonial, but concentrated on giving solid teaching, heard a few confessions, did a great deal with the youth of the district and was appointed as an assistant Diocesan Inspector of Schools.

Our rural dean, who lived nearby, was a weird bird - a naturist who ran about naked in all weathers in the garden of an early morning, lunching upon a handful of nuts and raisins. He always attended our weekday celebrations of Holy Communion, where a dozen communicants usually assembled, telling me that his flock were intractable and he despaired of doing such a thing there. Years later his church became quite "advanced" and mine fell away under later incumbents. No doubt I had not laid firm enough foundations, but my personal popularity had achieved apparent success. Here is a stern warning!

During the first half of my ministry there, the rectory was much improved and filthy drainage replaced. Noticing that a workman was hampered at his task of digging a channel by getting entangled with a rambler rose, I pushed the thorny branch aside and a dirty thorn pierced my finger. The result was a severe attack of "surgical scarlet". This almost cost me my life; but I was rushed to an Isolation Hospital in a fearful state. There, when on the mend, I was able to celebrate Holy Communion for the ward. The night sister, a Roman Catholic, acted as my server; so Easter Day was not neglected. This nurse and I had many a midnight feast upon cauliflower cheese, the vegetables being sent by my old gardener.

On my return I found that the villagers continued to skirt the rectory by going through the fields, lest they should catch "the fever" and I was so fat that I could not for some weeks play Rugger nor run with the young men. But I was able to drive round the diocese to inspect schools and to carry out my activities as assistant secretary of the Diocesan Missionary Council.

....

It was through attending a conference of the whole Church Missionary Council that I, until then regarded as a celibate, met my future wife. I had seen her, an assistant - secretary, at a smaller meeting in

Westminster and had felt a little interest in the attractive lady. This second meeting provided an opportunity for closer acquaintance. I noticed that she seemed worried over her housekeeping accounts concerning the crowd of guests. The figures would not tally. She thought that she ought to have more cash than there was in hand, having forgotten that she was not a guest but a paid official. My logical approach soon settled the matter.

After the little affair had been sorted, we walked and talked and she found some aspirin to soothe my nasty attack of sinusitis. On the morrow, the weather having improved, my senior colleague and I took her and her friend for an outing on the river. On our return to my car, she found that her handbag had disappeared and was rather distressed.

The following week I sent her an exact replica of her lost bag and my friend put a fountain pen inside. There followed a year's correspondence and visits between us to our respective homes and we were married by a friend of her family, a formidable bishop who chided me humorously after I had placed the ring on her finger, "Aren't you going to give her a chaste kiss? Go on, it's quite in order."

Of a very able mind, except possibly in mathematics, my dear wife though at first a nervous speaker became a Diocesan speaker for the Mothers Union, a first rate teacher of children and a story-teller, altogether a wonderful helpmate until her untimely death.

It came as a complete shock when our

bishop (urged by the rural dean, a previous vicar of the parish) pressed me to accept the charge of a huge slum-industrial complex. It was hard to leave our happy sphere and obey that call.

V "Just as words can do harm so also they can do good. Can I speak a word of praise or encouragement to somebody today?" (Thoughts. B.R.F.)

It is probably easier to gain an accurate view and have a more mature, balanced judgement of incidents which occurred years ago than to possess these faculties when they occurred. Though my first impression of our new sphere of work remains unchanged. I promised my bishop to serve there for five years. In return he said he would find me a decent living after that period.

The parish had been served by a weird assortment of clergymen. The first occupant of the vicarage had such fanatical views that he had the doors made so that the panels had no cross pieces - as if to say, "We abhor these things."

This oddity was followed by our rural dean who, not quite knowing why, removed the ugly deal table from before a fearsome pulpit, put the table to good use in the vestry, and set the pulpit in its usual position at the side and not the middle of the chancel arch. Then he had an altar made and set it upon steps in the Eastern Apse. At that point Kensitites made a disturbance and were ducked in the nearby horse trough by the churchmen.

There followed some men of learning, ability and genuine pastors; some cranks, and one or two mentally or physically pathological.

My preferment was, financially, one in reverse and the reason for my appointment obvious. Nobody wanted the job. Several had had a look and fled. The house was ugly, so was the church, the parish understaffed with only one assistant priest looking after two mission churches. A daughter church with an independent priest relieved the pressure by six thousand. But this left us with about fourteen thousand souls for whom to care.

From the very first, I could see little social distinction or educational difference between those attending the parish church and the two missions. Their separate existence merely meant dividing the workforce in face of little evidence that one mission had converted anybody during the forty years of running youth clubs, Social Services, clinics, entertainments and the Sunday worship attended by only those who ran the activities, that is as a general rule. The few who ever attended a service behaved in a listless fashion and I was told by the caretaker, when I conducted my first service there and remarked upon their general irreverence, "We just bends over."

At my suggestion, the bishop very kindly found the priest in charge - a man of almost my own age - a decent parish and sent an old Kelham trained man to assist me in addition to temporary help which I was being given by a Canadian clergyman.

Then a would-be deacon arrived, who had done me the honour of asking me to "give him a title" rather than his accepting one at a very famous church. Hindsight has made me wonder if the able young man thought he could manipulate my simple mind more easily than that of the other vicar. I may be quite unfair to him. But after all, he had no idea that my academic degree was no real indication of my actual mental powers, and his remarks might easily have been "snide" references to some of us clergymen who had not gained so good a degree as he had.

From the very first, this young man showed great organising ability, though as a mere deacon he could do little to help us when both myself and the senior man were down with influenza that first Christmas. But he quickly set to work and called upon some of the "Top Brass" of the diocese to come to our aid, telling them what to do. One of these canons spent a whole day in church conducting seven weddings.

After his "priesting", he became rather more self-assertive and occasionally the bishop rang me up and asked me to restrain him from upsetting the "City Fathers" and other influential people.

Despite this, we worked admirably as a team, much as a "Team Ministry" carries on today. The parish church-wardens were enthusiastic, and one said, "Nothing succeeds like success." But I was far from satisfied and made suggestions and plans for the future.

After settling which part of the parish each of us three should be responsible in visiting, I ruled that whether in the parish church or the mission the altar must be made the focus from which all went forth to serve God. To ensure that this was made clear, I insisted that Sung Eucharist in the parish church should be attended by all three priests in the hope that eventually the whole parish would attend this, instead of being split into three rather insignificant parts as at that time. The parish was thus organised after the manner of S. Mary Portsea.

This was not enthusiastically welcomed by our young colleague, who preferred to be "alone in his glory" - a case of divided authority, for his mission was under the patronage of a public school and the head had a "say" in what went on there, despite my overall authority. We were to see that what I suggested was precisely what the young fellow did when he later became my successor.

This Sung Mass was dignified by introducing the proper vestments and Holy Communion was celebrated daily by one of us in turn in a new Lady Chapel, which I had designed and which was built by a parishioner who only charged us for the cost of the materials used. I also obtained a "faculty" for reservation of the Blessed Sacrament in that chapel.

At this point I must pay a sincere tribute to our Lady Parish Worker, who made many vestments to supplement those generously given to us by the wife of a rich proprietor of a factory. The worker was a returned missionary from Central Africa, who helped us in the vicarage in the mornings, and spent the rest of the day at many parochial jobs. I therefore paid half of her salary and raised the remainder with some difficulty. She eventually left to train as a teacher and was succeeded by another young lady who was, I believe, still active when I was last in the parish at its centenary celebrations, and was photographed in the centre of a group of former priests who had served there. This included two bishops, but they treated me as the father of the family. My humanistic critic, mentioned below, was the first to welcome me.

Another worthwhile departure was making friends with the Free Church ministers without compromising our position. Very shy at first, they eventually joined with us at a monthly prayer meeting. My young colleague quarrelled with both the city missioner, calling him with some justification "The body snatcher" and with the R.C. priest with whom I was quite friendly and found co-operative.

My wife and I gathered together a dozen young men and women, one of them afterwards ordained priest, and we met weekly for a study with the object of training them to become leaders in the future congregation. The latter was until then mainly of middle-aged and elderly folks, so we held decorous Sunday evening gatherings after a well attended Evensong. Sometimes that meeting was used to discuss subjects of importance during Lent and more often we filled a large hall with young people from the streets and entertained them at community singing. This led to protests from a humanist neighbour and a visit from the bishop, who had his letter of complaint that we were singing bawdy music hall stuff, and we invited his lordship to come and join us.

From these efforts we gained many candidates for Confirmation, not merely from the crowds but rather by hand-picking likely ones from the seven hundred Sunday School children and those we saw occasionally in church. It has always been my policy to view people as individuals and not, as Socialists seem to do, in the mass. I can only love them in that way and not as a mere crowd.

Confirmation preparation was thorough and lengthy and candidates were strongly urged to use the Sacrament of Penance. My senior colleague was a skilled confessor, kept the females in order, while I undertook the hearing of confessions of boys and men. The junior did not excel at this type of work. He was fond of embarrassing practical jokes in which even the bishop fell a victim to his monkey tricks.

The work progressed so that a year before the outbreak of the 1939 war we had firmly established a parish Communion and vastly increased the number of communicants. Of this my junior was a keen advocate. At first he remained politically Conservative, having been secretary of that group of undergraduates at Cambridge. At that time he seemed to follow the notions of Samuel Smiles and his "Self Help" dicta. But our depressing area seemed to change him suddenly into a rabid 'Fellow Traveller' or extreme Socialist. So much so that the bishop asked me to restrain him a little.

His reaction was to try to persuade me either to follow his example or accept the offer of a more attractive parish, although he remained friendly and generously disposed towards me. I had no intention of doing either. God's call always faces us with a choice - to accept or reject. This was not long after he was "priested" and he had come to tell me he had been offered a college chaplaincy and asked whether he did rightly in turning it down. He continued to seek my guidance for several years. But on this occasion he unburdened himself of his aims, telling me that he would never accept the office of Suffragan Bishop, but that of a Diocesan was another matter.

Despite St. Paul's words to Timothy, "If a man desire the office of a Bishop he desireth a good work", I knew that the best priests of olden times had to be sought out from hiding places and almost forced to be consecrated when they heard that their canons had elected them to be bishops. I rather prefer that attitude.

The so-called "Phoney War" had little ill-effect upon our work and, when a National Government was formed, I suggested that it would be a good move to hear the voices of the three main political parties through the local M.P.s. Nothing was done about this at the time. But a seed was sown from which grew a mighty tree. I had rather not say whether it was the "Tree of Life" or that of the "Knowledge of good and evil".

Before all this, my old rector, whose family was distantly connected with my wife's and who was a cousin of Winston Churchill, came upon a visit and was much impressed by my young colleague. I have reason to believe that he mentioned him to the future Prime Minister when the latter came into power and the able young man's name "was put on the list", as the saying goes.

The beginning of the real conflict brought progress to a halt. But we did not "begin again at square one". When I went to the parish, on the first Sunday in Advent there were twelve communicants. We did not fall back so far as that, despite considerable evacuation taking place.

As a vicarage family, we had suffered serious illness. My wife's doctor diagnosed thyroid trouble, possibly cancerous if it developed. He told me to get her out of the place. She had suffered a severe operation for ectopic gestation. We had a boy of five just recovering from a nearly fatal attack of pneumonia, who had almost scalded himself to death when two years old. There was a toddler of nearly two years old. Both had not long thrown off severe whooping cough. A third child was on the way. Plenty of trouble at home!

During the severe air attacks that Autumn, my wife and the boys were taken out into the country in two different directions. Our doctor insisted that the family should settle in a country area for the sake of their health, so I was forced to the conclusion, unwelcome though it was, that we must make a move. Perhaps I *had* unwisely accepted the job as the young man said.

My bishop seemed to know nothing of our troubles, why I do not know, though he had troubles of his own. He admitted that I had served in that "hair shirt" parish for longer than I had promised, but could not keep his promise - he had little to offer but an exchange to a place almost next door to the parish where we had been so happy. "That would never do," said I, knowing what remarks I was likely to hear there about my successor. For it is almost always like that with "tittle tattle".

It was with no real regret that we left the horrible place, though leaving many loving people who told me with tears that we were running into danger by going to a village near the South Coast, for invasion was sure to come. Mr. Churchill's cousin had found us a quiet village down there. We kept Christmas in the home of a kindly parishioner and settled into our new vicarage in the New Year of 1941.

A great deal of this chapter may seem as though I am "blowing my own trumpet". I could write a long book about our life there. But I have picked out, as from my diaries, points which describe what I consider to be a sensible way of laying sound foundations upon which a successor can build, and I worked afterwards along these lines for more than a quarter of a century, for which I was given due credit.

This account may also dispel certain strange clouds of fiction, which have become rather a legend since those days of long ago.

VI "True wisdom is not limited to the prominent and powerful, nor even to the highly educated." (Thoughts. B.R.F.)

It was easy to fall a prey to scrupulosity, a typical Anglican spiritual disease endemic among those who never make a confession. My Spiritual Director soon settled it when I told him I was worried about being called to the village work. In fact, the place needed a priest. Formerly it had been served by a diocesan official, not demanding much attention, and not getting it.

My memory of that village street stands out clearly as I recollect feeling like Moses going in the sight of the people to enter the Tabernacle. That was what happened twice daily when I went to church to say morning and evening offices. I could almost feel their eyes boring into my back as they turned their heads watching my queer goings on when I went to say the daily services. They behaved just the same as I returned and merely grunted when I "passed the time of day", unlike my city workers who liked being spoken to by us cassock garbed priests.

In church, I found the figure of Christ had been taken from the Processional Cross, because the former incumbent found it too sad. I rescued it from our stables. After all, He was born in one. The people were accustomed to Mothering Sunday, when the children offered bunches of flowers saying, "For you-mer".

Early in my first year there, my senior colleague in the city had been made a canon and put in charge of the largest parish in the diocese for the duration of war. Our young man wrote, asking my advice as to whether he should accept the bishop's offer to make him vicar. "Yes," I replied. "if you will promise to stay at least ten years." He stayed fifteen and did some very fine work.

Introduction of a Sung Eucharist mid-weekly for the school and parents, at which the Methodist minister's son sometimes served, returning to the use of linen vestments, found in a cupboard, and restoring a Sung Eucharist as the principal morning service once a month, seemed to cause little fuss. But candles were more anathema than incense and we faced scurvy opposition until a vacancy occurred and I used subtlety in making my chief critic my new vicar's churchwarden. Then he fought my battles.

My chief job was to mediate between two rival gangs of ex-gypsies, the majority of the population. Then no enemy was left beyond a critic on the Church Council who asked me, "Why does Mr. X attend church no longer?" The meeting roared with glee when I replied, "I am not God who searches the hearts. But perhaps it is for the same reason as a certain man has for not speaking to his mother for the past six months." I could have added, "Thou art the man," but that was needless.

Another butt for village criticism was the schoolteacher who suffered a great deal from this disagreeable and exacting flock, which said that my wife and I had no business to beget children during the war.

They gave her £5 as a year's fee for helping in the parish. Dear me. What generosity!

We did all sorts of chores, ran a small-holding with goats and a pony, took in paying guests and pupils, to supplement our wretched living of less than seven pounds per week. On account of this, Madame Y's criticism of my toil-stained but scrubbed hands (so unlike those of her atheist son's) was the subject of a kindly but critical letter signed by my new bishop. Mr. Archdeacon, on being tackled, assured me that the bishop was angry and it was no use my going to see him.

In the face of such stupidity, I called on the dean, a friend of my wife's for many years, who told me that he had difficulty in keeping the peace of the close and advised me to ask the Suffragan Bishop how to get to see his lordship.

That chief assistant to our Father in God told me how difficult he himself found it to visit the bishop, and the ridiculous antics needed to achieve an interview. The substance of his instructions ran:-

"Go to the kitchen door and knock. Ask the cook, who will poke out her head, whether the bishop's niece is at home, or the domestic chaplain. If she says yes to either question, come away and try again. If she says no, then tell her you want to see the bishop. She will call up the stairs, his girl secretary will come down and take you up to see him. Got that?"

I carried out these instructions to the letter and was lucky, first time. The two watchdogs, hound and bitch, were absent and the girl told the bishop that a clergyman had arrived to see him. His reaction was pathetic. "Why can't I be allowed to see my clergy? I'm their Father in God. They should be free to call on me. How can I exercise my proper ministry?"

He had no recollection of the tiresome letter, but recognised me at once, saying, "I know you. I gave your children a ride in my car at the Confirmation in your 'Starving' of a parish. Have you come to ask for a better living? I'm sure you need and perhaps deserve one."

He then mentioned various possible moves until I pointed out that the offensive letter lay on his desk. "Ah well! Did I really sign that? It was all due to a wretched woman in your parish. She often writes to tell me how to run the diocese. You see, she was secretary or typist or something to a bishop in her younger days. Take no notice of her. I don't."

I then told him that I had quite recently heard of a suitable parish, from which the vicar sought to move into something smaller. Would he permit an exchange? He exclaimed, "Why are some of you best men leaving me?" I could have told him of his bossy niece and almost infidel chaplain, but thought it kinder to hold my tongue.

The truth was that having seen a notice in the Church Times, I had cycled over to see the place and talked to the vicar only the week before, after being in retreat. The income was worth twice what we were receiving. More to the point, the population was ten times as great and still increasing.

A life-work lay ahead.

Not quite easy in my conscience, I asked the Retreat Conductor and his reply was much to the point, "Would you be spiritually satisfied there?" I answered, "Not particularly. They are very protty."

"There you are!" he exclaimed. "Convert them. That's your call to serve there."

Then I called on my old friend to tell him of my opportunity. He said he could get me an important cure under the patronage of his cousin, Lord Z. But he did not advise this. In fact he had refused it himself. Later on I found that the archdeacon's nephew had been appointed to that living and afterwards climbed into a minor bishopric. I could hardly be blamed for imagining that, perhaps, that nasty letter was written to discredit me. But there are too many people with chips on their shoulders. Such an emcumbrance ill befits a priest.

VII "The seeker of God must be loving, direct, and honest with himself and others." (B.R.F.)
"Understanding is the reward of faith." (St. Augustine.)
"The man who has understanding has everything." (Jewish saying.)

Our new vicarage, the birth place of a famous canon of St. Paul's, was huge, so we let off part of it and further increased our income. At first there was opposition to the slightest change that I introduced, violent and aggressive in a few cases. In fact, I had to buy another car to visit in the far-flung parish and see patients in the distant hospitals. But my adversaries for a long time refused to grant any contribution towards expenses of that kind, whereas my successor now has a very satisfactory contribution.

It was five years before I was called anything but "The new vicar", who had introduced strange things. I had left everything alone for a year and then followed the lines adopted in the other town parish. The people said, "You'll get used to it", but I often spent a morning at golf to rid myself of the fug of their self-righteousness.

In those early days we also had a welcome from my young successor from the big town and we compared notes as usual and I gave what advice he asked for. Along with him came a coach-load of my old friends and we made merry together.

I paid a return visit and found the

Blessed Sacrament reserved on the Lady Altar and that night we had Benediction with eighty young people present, most of whom I knew by name.

Years later, when the able young man had moved to a more important cure (if any is more so than another, which is doubtful), I was again invited to speak and found between a hundred and fifty to two hundred at the parish Communion. Nearly all of them had been prepared for Confirmation and trained by our old team of three.

Within a few years, the young man's desire was fulfilled and he was given a bishopric which was not everyone's dream.

....

My own parish began to wake up when an "old-timer" returned from overseas. He was unhelpful at first when he joined forces with a "Paisleyite" type "Brass Hat" Serviceman, in complaining about my Romish tendencies. For instance, he assured me that nobody would attend Midnight Mass at Christmas. Over a hundred came and year by year numbers increased.

We had a monthly Sung Eucharist for our growing Sunday School and the parents, well over a hundred. The Eucharist was sung at 11 a.m. one Sunday in the month, Matins being said at 10.30 a.m. on that day. Very soon the "old-timer" was the only one present.

Eventually he saw through the Paisleyite's humbug and even approved of my changes. He considered that the Easter ceremonies were beautiful, having seen them in the Holy Land, but thought they were beyond our people's grasp. He was probably right.

Music was, of course, one of my great concerns and it was not always easy to deal with our mixed choir. A Servers Guild was a success. Other work with youths, boxing and athletics was linked with an afternoon class, working well until picketed by some wretched lads.

Regarding youth work, I am afraid that "starry eyed" clergymen are sometimes deceived by the charm of undesirable men who creep unawares into posts such as organists and youth workers. One may actually come along with the blessing of leaders of the Boy Scouts, who say the man is suitable - "quite sound, though difficult to get along with." That happened once and ruined one promising field of work. I am afraid that I found it difficult to help offenders of that kind.

....

To return to the subject of my one-time colleague - at the time of his elevation to the Bench of Bishops, there flourished for a short period a Church Pictorial. Its editor made a great to-do about our young hero, stressing what great things he had done in going to a squalid city parish, with its ugly church and feebly despondent people (or words to that effect, almost calling the folks "depraved"). The article read as though the brilliant young man had done everything himself, turning everything upside down. But its writer might plead that he really meant that this work had begun when the man went there as a deacon.

I was taken aback by this somewhat specious article, as few knew the man as well as I did. A later archbishop's tart rejoinder, when the young bishop criticised him, was that had he been archbishop then, my friend would not have been made a bishop. Rebuilding war-wreckage, gathering three congregations into one, fifteen years hard work as vicar called for more than silly journalism.

Upset by the "puff" contained in the article, I felt very ready to agree with that archbishop and this resulted in a comic encounter with my own bishop in our cathedral city.

He approached me and exclaimed, "Aren't you basking in the reflected glory of your old curate being made a bishop? I must elevate you, I can see."

My reply was, "Huhh, indeed." So I was not made an honorary canon and accordingly was not put to the expense of paying the fee demanded on installation to such questionable dignity.

But priests must learn to control the tongue and remember that it is the work that matters, not who did it, and it is Christ's Church and not Father or Mr. A's Church that stands by the roadside.

Though embarrassed at a Toc H rally not long after, when the Lord Mayor introduced me to a cadet member of the Royal Family as "The man who really did most of the work and should have been made a bishop," the hurt was somewhat relieved. That remark was somewhat unjustified, for the man had done a fine job, staying there for fifteen years; but both the mayor and the new bishop were able to make enemies as readily as friends, which probably explains the outburst.

My irritation was also mollified in later years by the way another diocesan bishop thanked me on two occasions for the way in which I must have trained and influenced the bright lad. "I should never have been a bishop but for his influence," he declared. "Therefore you are in some way responsible too." Never a similar word of appreciation came from my former colleague. Perhaps he thought I did not deserve one.

....

Any idea of his success is not often possible for a parish priest unless he stays there for about twenty years and begins to marry those whom he once baptised. This had begun to happen when my dear wife's early death almost broke me in mind and body, so I retired, to quote my bishop's words, "In a blaze of glory." (Not the "basking" bishop!)

Soon recovering from my distress, I might then have been of more use in some humble diocesan capacity than in premature retirement. But it pleased me to hear that this bishop had been asked by the Church Council to appoint some priest of similar views to mine, and the congregation at my successor's institution heard the bishop tell him to follow on with the good work that I had done. I have visited the parish since and know that he is doing just that.

CONCLUSION

"For if our virtues
Did not go forth of us, "twere all alike
As if we had them not..." (Shakespeare.)

The urge to obey the call and serve has induced me to give freely of my services for weekday celebrations of Holy Communion. But I now feel that, with the rising cost of living and maintaining a motor car, we retired clergy should accept the proper fees for duty. I have not come to this conclusion without regret.

When I spent three months in Africa a few years ago, I addressed the Lusaka Theological College upon the subject of this essay and found the African ordinands very aware that the Holy Spirit may move a man to serve the Church through the priesthood.

Not an old fogey, I can say by heart all the words of Series II of the Revised Liturgy, have no bigoted objection to Series III, excepting the possibility of insincerity when "Passing the Peace" in addition to shaking hands entering and leaving the church, and, perhaps, for the fourth time at coffee afterwards. The old Liturgical Embrace was far and away better, though awkward.

Some of the popular 100 hymns seem to me ridiculous, after the fashion of "Gert and Daisy." One verse of "Lord of the Dance" appears to me rather blasphemous, picturing Christ dancing as he suffered the agonies of Crucifixion. Had the word's author any idea of what that awful death entailed? I hope it can be rephrased without spoiling the hymn - otherwise good.

Yes, I am rather censorious, hate and avoid chapter meetings and almost as bad as an old canon in my last parish - a thorn in my side. "Mea culpa"

BENEDICITE SACERDOTES DOMINI DOMINO